EXPLODING
CHIPPEWAS

EXPLODING CHIPPEWAS

MARK TURCOTTE

TriQuarterly Books
NORTHWESTERN UNIVERSITY PRESS
EVANSTON, ILLINOIS

TriQuarterly Books
Northwestern University Press
www.nupress.northwestern.edu

Printed in the United States of America

10 9 8 7 6 5 4

ISBN 978-0-8101-5122-2 (cloth)
ISBN 978-0-8101-5123-9 (paper)

Library of Congress Cataloging-in-Publication Data
Turcotte, Mark.
    Exploding Chippewas / Mark Turcotte.
        p. cm.
    ISBN 0-8101-5122-7 (alk. paper) — ISBN 0-8101-5123-5 (pbk. : alk. paper)
    1. Indians of North America—Poetry. 1. Title.
    PS3570.U627 E97 2002
    811'.54—dc21

                                                2002001619

The section "Road Noise" was written as my part of a word/music
collaboration with Chicago composer and bassist Mitar Mitch Covic.
Moments of "Road Noise," in slightly different versions, first appeared
in *The Feathered Heart* (revised edition, Michigan State University
Press, 1998).

For remembering, for not forgetting.

CONTENTS

Thanks to Mike Puican, in whose Chicago kitchen many of these poems were written. Thanks to LeRoy's Water Street Coffee for the friendly space to scribble.

Grace and blessings to my family and to Ma & Pa Presnell, Mitar Covic, Steve Grutzmacher, Eric Gansworth, Steve Kastner, Fred Alley, Quraysh Ali Lansana, Ray Gonzalez, Adrian C. Louis, and Dominique Falkner. Your support and encouragement have been vital.

Thanks to Brian Schram, Bill Schutte, and the rest of the boys in the lumberyard, and to Kenny Honold for teaching me how to operate the Boom Truck.

Heavy thanks to Tony Fitzpatrick for the beauty and danger in his scratching.

Special thanks to Reg Gibbons for his friendship and counsel.

Love to my brother, Ronald C. Pant. We all miss you. Don't trip over your wings.

And big love to Kathleen and Ezra for your patient and loving hearts.

I am grateful to the Wisconsin Arts Board for its encouragement during the creation of this book, and to the Lannan Foundation for its tremendous support during, and now beyond, its completion.

EXPLODING
CHIPPEWAS

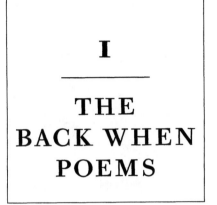

I

THE BACK WHEN POEMS

FIRST INDIAN:
The scar on my lip? Oh, I got that
when I was a kid on the rez.
That's where I got most of my scars.
At least the ones you can see.

SECOND INDIAN:
Yes, on the rez, back when you
used to be Indian.

(FIRST INDIAN *and* SECOND INDIAN *both laugh.*)

CONTINUE

Back when I used to be Indian
I am reaching toward the light
with both fists, yawning,
growling like a flower.
Mother pushes me, gasping.
Mother pushes me again.
I swim out from muffled
cradle, dripping blood,
salt of the very first
flood, first wound, I uncurl
upon the island shore.
I breathe.
Mother pulls me, gasping.
Mother pulls me again
to her weeping breast. I drink
and begin, with one shaky eye,
to search for my father.
The room rattles with empty.
In the hallway hoofbeats fade.
Millions cry in my veins.

GRAVITY

Back when I used to be Indian
I am counting the stars
in the night of my mother's eyes.
Five, four, three.
Her husband is heaped in the corner,
chains rattling in his throat.
She groans and lifts herself
finally from the floor. A bone explodes
in her neck. She begins to spin.
Two, one.
The darkness pulls me.
Another glowing cinder drops
out of the sky.

VISITATION

Back when I used to be Indian
I am six maybe seven
years old, restless, pretending to sleep
in the dry glow of the cast-iron
stove. My sister's back is warm
and still against my own.
A straw in the blanket scratches my ankle.
Somewhere in the darkness
my mother and her husband grunt
and hiss, hands over mouths.
I blink.
Across the room a buffalo snorts,
nudges the yellow Tonka truck
with its nose.

BATTLEFIELD

for Jackie

Back when I used to be Indian
I am standing outside the
pool hall with my sister.
She, strawberry blond. Stale sweat
and beer through the
open door. A warrior leans on his stick,
fingers blue with chalk.
Another bends to shoot.
His braids brush the green
felt, swinging to the beat
of the jukebox. We move away.
Hank Williams falls again
in the backseat of a Cadillac.
I look back.
A wind off the distant hills lifts my shirt,
brings the scent
of wounded horses.

HARVEST

Back when I used to be Indian
I am squinting into the sun
where a great bird is disappearing.
The furrows of the field
stretch out to a darkening
horizon. The People, every shade
of brown, stoop to dig potatoes
from the earth.
Armando sits astride the sputtering
tractor, his long black fingers
wrapped around a bottle
of bright orange soda.
He grins, his mouth filled
with gaps and gold,
offers down a drink.
I take a sip.
The heavens cough and let loose
the storm. A jagged tooth slides
down my throat. Between the drops
of rain, feathers fall in flames.

AWAY

Back when I used to be Indian
I am listening to the white world,
sunken in the strange smell
of my new bed. Across the city
the Lansing Drop Forge chomps
at the night. Big bites out of thick
moonlight. Sirens like dying crows.
Distant dogs yap and whine.
A breeze scrapes at the window
screen. I pull the blanket tight
to my neck, my hair rustles against
the pillow. Heart shudders.
I close.
It is not the wind that scratches
its dark and furry back along the walls
of our house, throws long shadows,
grunts and sniffs beneath the door.
The *rugaru* surrounds my dreams,
carries ghosts on its breath
to beckon me home.

GROW

Back when I used to be Indian
I am scratching it all down, pen
clawing paper like a fevered bird.
Everything is wing and word.
Shiny seeds fall out of my hair,
tumble over the worn edges
of the rickety card table. Sunlight
slants through dust. A tiny bead
of blood drops from my eye, splatters
into stars on the floor. Monsters
and angels pop from the linoleum,
rise in the air perched on blue
petals and rosy thorns. Long vines
wrap and moan around my legs.
I disappear.
In the kitchen Mother scrubs pots
and pans, wipes sweat from her brow,
calls for me to take out the trash.
Waits. Calls again. A garden
moves in her living room,
wind stirs her hair.

TWIST

for Zapp

Back when I used to be Indian
I am sixteen maybe seventeen
years old, drugged, driving the back
gravel roads with the white
boys, trunk filled
with beer. We close our hundredth
circle and park on the shining
tractor path at the edge
of a frosted field.
Thunder heavy from
the cassette deck.
Kevin bangs his head, babbling.
In the dew of his breath
on the window glass Steve traces
the names of all the girls he
wants to fuck. A door slams.
I wake up.
Upon his hands and knees Johnny
vomits algebra, football, and
prom queens. I wrap him in my
jacket, carry him back to the car.
A deer staggers into our headlights,
an arrow through its neck. The blade
in my pocket dances against
my hip, digs in, begins to whisper
to my mixed
up blood.

BOOM

Back when I used to be Indian
I am leaning into the shadows,
my shoulder against the rough
mud and log wall. The old
woman's fingers mumble
down the length of her black
rosary, her head haloed against
the chimney of a kerosene lamp.
In his box, resting across two weathered
sawhorses, Uncle Big Tooth frowns
in his new dream. A fat fly scratches
at the leather of his chin as the tiny
crucifix sways above the silver lids
of his lightless eyes. The mourners
all swoon to the invisible, tongues
in muffled rhythm. Drums from
somewhere build a heat.
I explode.
Big Tooth rises, leaps to the dusty
floor. He shakes his throat,
stomps a trail of stars out
the door and into the sky.
Everything is a circle and all
that is not Indian in the World
suddenly disappears.

SIGNAL

for Jim Mottonen

Back when I used to be Indian
I am climbing down through the dark
ravines with my best friend, Billy.
We prowl the deep cuts until just
out of sound of the rampaging
dormitories. Straddling a fallen
tree, we trade swigs from a flask
of wine, draw breath, and listen.
Above us, in the vast black beyond
the swaying tips of bursting branches,
string tangled in the trees, our yellow
kite flaps in a hard wind. Billy grins
and whispers, *three days, three nights.*
In a nearby field two lovers gaze
at the sky, imagine a ghost, a UFO.
I look up.
Murmuring, Billy remembers being
a boy frozen by spidery
shadows on his bedroom curtain.
I remember hands like webs. He takes
the flask from my fingers.
The string is still taut.
We haven't been to class in days.
No one has noticed.

BURN

Back when I used to be Indian
I am crushing the dance floor,
jump-boots thumping Johnny Rotten
Johnny Rotten. Red lights blue bang
at my eyes. The white girl watching
does not know why and it doesn't matter.
I spin spin, eat I don't care for breakfast,
so what for lunch. She moves to me,
dark gaze, tongue hot to lips. The music
is hard, lights louder. She slides low
against my hip to hiss, *go go Geronimo.*
I stop.
All silence he sits beside the fire
at the center of the floor, hands stirring
through the ashes, mouth moving in the shape
of my name. I turn to reach toward him,
take one step, feel my skin begin
to flame away.

FLOOD

Back when I used to be Indian
I am cutting glances through the tiny
squares of the window screen down
into the street. Up and down the walls
of a city that I must leave, the light
goes on changing. Yellow red green
to yellow and yellow. The rain keeps
falling, caution rising as evening pales.
Winter in San Francisco is murky cold.
Billy's been sick for days, swimming
for his life. The broken umbrella
leans in the corner. Our last can of tuna
waits for a loaf of bread. My lungs fill
with brick and pavement, taxicabs.
I sink.
It would be better to be living back
in the park, setting the beach on fire again
with all her names. A woman maybe
a girl far away. I would call the storm,
dare lightning to strike, if only
I knew that she
would rescue me.

REFLECTION

for Isaiah Drew

Back when I used to be Indian
I am twenty-six maybe twenty-seven
years old, exhausted, walking the creek
that bends through the hills
down into the clattering mesquite.
Along the muddy bank
I search for any sign
of my family. Footprints, feathers,
blood. A smoldering campfire
sours in my nose. *Mojados.*
Yellow pencil shavings curl
in the warm ash. *Poetas.*
A circle of sun floats
and spreads across the water.
I step in.
Murky bottom rises
over my boots, swirls,
and swallows up the light.
As I kneel to speak
a long black bird bursts
from my throat.

MOTION

Back when I used to be Indian
I am holding the words deep
in my throat. The black and
silver Mustang slices
silently toward an ancient orange
West Texas sky. The steering wheel
shakes and hums in my hands
like a dowsing stick. The sun
is a bruise on the horizon.
In the distance pump-jacks peck
relentless at the earth.
To left and right the world
is a blur of endless fences
draped with coyote skins.
Flexing my fingers I glance
over at her soft brown
knees. This is the place.
I cough.
Maria laughs, stars spin from
her teeth as night encircles us
with sound. Wings, howling.
She throws her arms around
my neck and everything
is swallowed.

CALL

Back when I used to be Indian
I am stretching out beneath
her, the thin white curtains
waving like wings above
our bed. The drowsy bird
of me unfolds into her hands.
She grins, crawls over me, shakes
her head. The long black
feathers of her hair fall between
my teeth as I rise
into her dark and trembling hips.
Against the wall Jesus
dangles from his cross, eyes
searching for the sky.
I hear children out in the yard.
They chase chickens in circles of laughter,
while in the shade of a ragged pecan
tree Abuela is coughing, grinding
the corn into dust, muttering,
oh Dios mío, Dios mío.
I rise again.
A table in the corner begins
to shudder. Over and over she falls
upon me. The eyes of Jesus.
The ceiling cracks open. Angels and
adobe crash into the room.

GO

Back when I used to be Indian
I am gripping the wheel with both
fists, plunging headlights northward
out of a long and syrupy night.
Texas behind me. The Anadarko Basin,
Will Rogers Turnpike, behind me.
Tulsa and the Jesus radio. Praise be.
I leave one thousand ghosts howling
in the rearview mirror. The dank
honky-tonks behind me. Easy heated
flesh, flickering tongues forked with poison.
Empty hands. Boot-scootin' rodeo queens
stagger in red taillight glow.
I stop to fill 'er up, drowse over one last
plate of biscuits with sausage gravy.
Bottomless cup of coffee and gone again.
Just west of St. Louis a nodding
hitchhiker catches me with his sign.
MOTHER FUNERAL DETROIT.
As he climbs in I say, *man, you can
sleep all the way to Chicago.*
Ahead, the pavement shimmers,
ancient Mississippi flows.
I cross over.
Silent sun and morning dew
make grassy stars. The hum of rubber
on the road, telephone poles.
Lines lead to lines to the edge
of the city, where we both wake up.
Praise be. I swear I hear poets
singing on the radio.

DRAW

for Kathleen

Back when I used to be Indian
I am waiting for her to find
me. Thunder from out of the throat
of the night. The air sizzles,
lightning singes all the rooftops
of the city. Rain bangs at every
window, seeps into the mortar
of every brick and dream.
The sheets beneath me are soaked
with memory. The storm
loud and electric. She paces
in her rooms. The pencil
falls from her fingers, the paper
floats to the floor.
I smile.
Tips of wings tap tap at her
ankles, circles of light braid
her hair. She presses an ear
to the wall, her hips to the wall.
My laughter. She peers into
the hallway, nearly nearly
knocks at my door.

CONTACT

for Ezra Cole

Back when I used to be Indian
I am humming into the soft
new ear of my son. He clings
to me, the world, with balled
fists, the knot of his cord
pressing into the flesh
of my wet and rising belly.
We bask in the pure
human heat of beginning.
His mama showers away
the sweat and labor
of twenty-one hours,
while other women change
the bedding, brew tea.
I drift.
In the near darkness she whispers
our names. Windows fly open.
Wings drum air. Three candles
stutter. The Old Ones crowd
the room, their chattering thick,
strange, and familiar. My hands on
fire I lift him to her, the moon
growing in her eyes.

NEAR

Back when I used to be Indian
I am thirty-six maybe thirty-seven
years old, calm, watching wife
and son frolic at the edge
of the big water. They bend together,
finger bright stones, shells, tiny
fish bones. He digs with his toes.
Everything is a treasure. She smiles
deeply, hair wrapped in wind around
the fine curve of her hip, lifts the hem
of her dress and ties it at her knees.
Hand in hand, they move away,
waltzing in the wet sand. Moon
on gradual waves. Other wings
against the dusk of sky. Their footprints
glow golden before me, lead to the shape
of them, vague and round as one.
I follow.
On a ridge above the beach, among feathery
pines, creatures stir and gather
with shiny eyes. He says, *look Mama look.*
She hushes a finger to her lips.
Laughter, growling.

TELL

for Mick Vranich

Back when I used to be Indian
I am sitting in a booth in a late
night café, Chicago draped around
me like anxious, wasted breath.
Across the shiny tabletop Raven
leans toward his coffee, wrapping
the white cup with long
fingers hardened from bending
over sawhorses and hammering
guitars. Music of nails. Words fall out
of his ears. Words rise from his boots.
Words spin the forks and spoons.
He shakes his head back into silky
shoulders, begins to sing, *brother
brother.* His feathers scrape
the plates from the tables, bang
against the fluorescent lights.
I whirl.
Out in the street, hooves clatter
over the hoods of cars, claws scratch
the backs of wobbling trains. The story is old.
The umph of his soul and the waitress
running to his wings.

EXIT

Back when I used to be Indian
I am falling toward my
face in the bathroom mirror.
It is a year maybe
a moment ago. My wife lies
back in the tub, eyes clenched tight,
cheeks carved with the cuts
of one thousand tears.
Scalding water rages from the faucet,
steam rises in the room.
Another fat moon
of milk hangs from her nipple,
waiting for a mouth.
I crash in.
Silvery shards break on my teeth.
Blood tastes of baby's breath. Milk
overflows onto the floor, rushes
over my feet. We both scream.
I do not reach for the door.
Everything everything sounds
like cooing.

ORBIT

Back when I used to be Indian
I am pushing my fingers
along the crooked darkness
of my mother's spine. Moonlight
on snow through the window.
The room is stiff with camphor.
My hands cramp in the heat of her pain.
Eighty-three winters of nothing
quite right. She mumbles into
the pillow like a child.
I coo to her, reach with my
heart through my glowing palms.
Little boy. The roof creaks
under an agony of wind.
I pray.
She sits up to find me at
my knees, moves shaky fingers
to my hair, pulls me. I want to say
that I am sorry sorry. She shushes
me, listening. I begin to spin.
She thinks she hears
a baby crying.

II

ROAD NOISE

for our sons

EZRA COLE
who is loved and cherished

and

ISAIAH DREW
who is loved and missed

INTRODUCTION

In late October of 1992 I received a message from a hospital in Fargo, North Dakota, telling me that they had the body of my father. They had tracked me down by beginning with a phone number found in his wallet, tracing me through this and that relative. They told me that they needed to speak with a next-of-kin before making plans for some kind of burial. I had, since I was a very young boy, grown up without this man they were calling my father. I had only had contact with him three times over the next thirty years, and hadn't seen him at all in the last twelve. Despite that lack of contact, I agreed, in the moment of the phone call, to travel to Fargo to oversee the burial.

A few days later, as Bill Clinton was being elected for the first time, I found myself on the Turtle Mountain Reservation, near the Canadian border and in the midst of a fierce snow and ice storm. Standing on the steps of the church, I realized that I was about to say goodbye to a man who had somehow, even from a distance, had a deep impact on my life.

It's a story not about sadness, but about power.

ELECTION DAY I

As America was stirring from its usual slumber,
I stood on the ice-encrusted steps
of the church at St. Ann's Mission.
        It was Election Day 1992,
a stark and stormy North Dakota morning.
Shivering in my too-thin coat,
cupping a match to another cigarette,
I watched the cars filled with mourners
grind up the slippery hill.

Below me, the men
were struggling with the weight of the long gray box,
their thick brown hands cracking open in the freezing air
as they huffed up the steps,
shuffled past me,
and were swallowed up into the church.

As the heavy doors closed behind me,
there was a sudden burden of breath upon my neck,
sweet and musty warm.
The wind rose swirling snow about my legs.
The trees in the yard began to shake,
the brittle branches clacking together, clicking together, clicking,
click click, click click, click click.

ROAD NOISE I

The story of your skin,
it echoes along the steel-ice rails
that run like black-blood veins over the heart of America,
shivers beneath the screeching wheels of lumbering engines.
The rocking boxcars are haunted by the dreams you left behind,
    that howling.
The freight yards ring with the ghost songs of men like you.

Men like you,
who as boys,
jumped the trains to escape the farmers and their fields,
    the forced labor,
the hands that held the whips that burned the welts into your backs.

Men like you,
who as boys,
a generation after Wounded Knee,
a generation after the assassination of Sitting Bull,
    lived with all that blood screaming in your ears,
all that blood running down your backs,
all of that stinging.

Men like you,
who as boys,
grieved for the thunder of the herds,
dreamed of the thunder of the ponies and their hooves,
    that howling.

Men like you,
who as boys,
sought out, discovered, and created
    road noise.

FISTS AND FINGERS DREAM

A man can be so many things,
hard and cold and soft and warm and tender.
A man can be smooth as a blade,
jagged at the edge.
His eyes can draw you in,
cut you open wide to please his teeth.
A man can be so many things,
a sinner or a saint,
anything that fists or fingers can dream.

    The thing about him was his voice.
    Glory, he was angel tongued. Devil, he was
    like Lucifer with that laugh that made you reach
    for a rosary. He had the most gentle hands,
    stroking my hair that day on the porch,
    humming one of them Indian songs.
    He's the one, that's him,
    he was saying *candy* and then his big hand was up
    and under and I. . . .

When he caught that woman who jumped from the window of
    the burning building,
he was sixty years old, got an award from the police.
He hit that cop so hard, even his wife,
afterward,
didn't recognize his face.
I saw him once empty his pockets to all those drunks outside the
    tavern,
gave 'em everything he had.
Two months with him and there was nothing left,
but us in the street, and him never looking back.

My kids, they loved him,
jumped all up and down when he came around.
He slapped that little boy on the ass till he was either gonna piss
    or bleed.
Potty training.
He had it hard, you know, his mama saying
he was someone else's child, not even hers.
He gave it hard, you know, left behind so many bruises,
so many bodies,
so much wreckage.

A man can be so many things,
broken or beautiful,
strong or lonely.
Damaged, damned, and angry.
Resurrected.
Forgiven or forgotten.
A man can be so many things,
a sinner or a saint,
anything that fists or fingers can dream.

ROAD NOISE II

For men like you,
the rhythm in the rails leads to
the hiss of desert highways laid out flat,
edge of earth to edge of earth,
everything and nothing in between.
From Flagstaff to Needles to Barstow,
snapping lizard tongues,
dried-up armadillos,
the devil's playground,
everything and nothing in between.
Juke joints, truck stops, cup o' coffee cup o' coffee.
Revival Lighthouse Palace of Christ,
speak in tongues for a bowl o' soup bowl o' soup.
You mop a floor,
peel off a pair of fishnets,
pick a pocket, and level that thumb again
over the heated strip of tar and dreams,
        that howling.

Slice your way through the north country,
the hum of the roads walled in forests,
far as the eye can see,
tree line to tree line,
everything and nothing in between.
From Duluth to Chicago to Detroit,
belching factories,
rotten-egg rivers,
the rust-belt grind,
everything and nothing in between.
Juke joints, truck stops, cup o' coffee cup o' coffee.

Salvation Army bread lines,
sing a hymn for a bowl o' soup bowl o' soup.
You wash a dish,
bust a head,
then go to jail, listening to the wheels whining in your bones,
    father highway calling.

ELECTION DAY II

As America was stirring from its usual slumber,
I stood on the ice-encrusted steps
of the church at St. Ann's Mission.
I crushed the butt of my cigarette
beneath the toe of my new dress shoe,
tightened and straightened the knot of my tie,
and turned to enter into the church,
into the dim light of death and murmuring.
> *There he is, that's Andy's boy,*
> *don't you know he looks like Andy's boy.*

As they all looked to me, searching my face for a sign,
I nodded, floating between the pews.
They all looked to me.

The long gray box was open and waiting at the other end of the room.
The long gray box was open and vibrating at the other end of the room.
The long gray box was open and laughing at the other end of the room.
My hands began to remember.
> There once was a sunny day, big water.
Then suddenly I was heavy to the floor,
the aisle stretched out before me like another endless highway,
a pavement hot and sticky with blood beneath my heels.
My hands began.
At the other end of the room the long gray box was open and
> spinning,
the needle in a mad compass
every direction pointing to every direction.

My hands,
      the box was open,
began to remember,
      the box was open,
I hated you,
      the box was open,
I denied you,
      the box was open,
I waited for you,
      the box was open,
I looked for you,
      the box was open,
I loved you,
      the box was open and spinning,
and they were all looking to me,
searching my face for a sign,
and my hands began to remember.

ROAD NOISE III

Father highway calling,
the wheels whining in your bones,
everything and nothing in between.
Only the road noise in your head,
your blood always remembering,
your blood always reminding you
there is no way to get away.
Because the story of your skin was written in the wind of wounded horses,
and the world never wanted to hear that noise.
The noise of men like you.
The world didn't want to know and would not know and could not know.
So, they give you thirty days in the hole,
bread and water bread and water,
over and over, again and again.

No, America doesn't want to hear that noise.
They just want to make it,
and louder.
Their chugging engines to muffle the sound of their cannons.
Their clanking factories to drown the sound of Chippewa children
        falling in the snow.
The hiss of machines to bury the sound of bad medicine hidden
        in the weave of blankets.
The boiling pots of rancid meat,
the maggots twisting in a plate of beans,
        I mean,
they don't want to hear.
Not even the noise they make,
the noise they gave to men like you.
The noise to be

born with
raised with,
to live with
to love with
hurt with
hate with
create with
kill with,
the noise of men like you,
pacing in your cells rocking
on your heels shadowboxing,
       boxing all the shadows,
always in motion,
always the father highway calling,
always holding your hands over your ears,
tearing at your hair, saying,
stop it stop it stop it
it hurts oh God God God it hurts
you hurt me
God, you hurt me,
you let them hurt me with their God,
with all that noise.

The story of your skin is told in the rumblings that shiver through you,
in the endless hall of echoes,
stretching through you like a road,
winding deeper and deeper back into the forests of men like you,
forests filled with the ghost songs of men like you.
And through your blood,
men like you,
leave the noise to ring in the ears
of men like me.

DUST

Little boys, they sure do love their daddies,
look up to their daddies,
they want to walk like their daddies,
they want to talk like their daddies, too,
they want to try their feet inside his shoes.
Don't you know,
they love to hear, *someday you're gonna be big just like your daddy.*
Little boys, they love to fall into his wide grin,
love to be lifted in his hands,
      higher than the trees.
And they love to watch him dance with Mama,
to hold her safe and tight,
to listen to him hum and strum guitar, singing songs to Mama,
just like Johnny Cash, singing, *flesh and blood needs flesh and blood,*
      and you're the one I need.
Like Jim Reeves's or Hank Locklin's "Four Walls,"
     out where the bright lights are glowing,
     you're drawn like a moth to a flame,
     you laugh while the wine's overflowing,
     while I sit and whisper your name.
Little boys, they sure do love their daddies.

    The child was struck,
    at a tender age,
    with the dry-mouth taste of his father's dust.
    The dust of lies, the dust of rage, the dust of wandering, the going away.
    The child was struck,
    gasping for air,
    parched and choking
    on the memory growing in his throat.
    For his father made the earth shudder beneath the fall of his foot.

His father made other men tremble beneath the gust of his voice.
The dust of lies, the dust of rage, the dust of wandering, the going away.
For his father ate the sky with his teeth,
and with his hands dragged deep scars
into the flesh of hearts, the flesh of backs, the flesh of minds,
        into the flesh of dreams.

For his father was the first
to bruise the child
with the fist of his patience,
to rape the child
with the body of shame,
to sting the child
with the tongue of hate.
The dust of lies, the dust of rage, the dust of wandering, the going away.

The child was struck,
at a tender age,
with the dry-mouth taste of his father's dust,
for his father was the first
to make the child want to spit.

You laugh while the wine's overflowing,
while I sit and whisper your name.
Little boys, they sure do love their daddies,
always trying to be like Daddy,
trying to find Daddy in their own eyes.
Always trying to find Daddy,
        to find Daddy.
And daddies, don't you know, they love their little boys.

ROAD NOISE IV

Through your blood,
men like you
leave the noise to ring
in the ears of men like me.
And that's all you ever gave,
that noise,
taut wires snapping in my veins.
All you ever gave to me is the need to kill the noise with more noise,
to walk away and walk away,
to heed the call of father highway,
      the call of highway father.

For you, the four walls were the four directions stretching endlessly,
everything and nothing in between.
And I learned it right away.
At three years old I hit the road,
and when they realized I was gone,
      they caught up with me a mile and a half away,
and I told them I was going to find my daddy,
because I needed to find my daddy.
When they realized I was gone.

Still, I swore I was never gonna be like you.
But I was angry,
I was hopeless.
I couldn't touch, I couldn't feel anything or anyone.
I swore I was never gonna be like you.
But all the while my wheels were turning,
I was on that road,
spinning and spinning.

43

I was thirteen and driving so fast and so far into my core
that I saw nothing but the blur of passing landscapes.
I was seventeen and driving so fast and so far out of myself
that I knew nothing but pure light, a blinding light.
I was twenty-five and driving, hit-and-run, leaving a few bodies behind, now.
I was thirty and driving, leaving a few dreams behind, a little more of myself
        behind.
And when they realized I was gone,
caught me a lifetime and a half away,
crawling along the shoulder of the road,
I told them I was going to find my daddy,
because I needed to find my daddy,
to look into his eyes, to ask him,
        why, why do I need to be like you?

THE WAITING

And while you were growing old in Fargo,
I was growing weary.
Waiting for you,
el Indio on the side of the road,
waiting in those wide-open West Texas nights.
Even standing perfectly still, I answered the call of father highway,
staring up at the stars, driving deeper and deeper into my own night,
the earth turning beneath me,
      the thundering herds, the ponies and their hooves,
all that blood screaming in my ears,
saying, *you are he you are he you are he.*

All that blood,
my hands shaking
      opening and closing,
trying to reach out.

     I was *el Indio*
     the night of the dance.
     Down along the border whirling,
         I watched her whirl to Tejano guitars,
     while golden beckoning birds
     flew from beneath her shimmering skirt.

     My tequila fingers,
     reaching for her,
     trapped a bird within her hem,
         ripped the glimmering thread,
     and she looked at me
     as though I
     had torn the moonlight in half.

While you were dying in Fargo,
I was exhausted.
My hands empty,
el Indio waiting on the side of the road,
walking the mesquite desert
looking for any sign of my family,
      footprints, feathers, blood,
my bones so noisy, now, that there was nothing but sound,
white noise at fever pitch,
all those voices telling me, *you are he you are he.*

And then there was nothing left
      but the sputtering candle.
The monster of my face in the bottom of the glass,
      the noise.
The night the bullet the pistol the finger and the trigger,
and me never looking back.
I was *el Indio,* waiting for you to set me free,
      when the telephone rang,

there was a whispering,
saying, *you are he you are he you are he.*

ELECTION DAY III

As America was stirring from its usual slumber,
I was moving down the aisle of the church at St. Ann's Mission.
They were all looking to me,
searching my face for a sign.
Before me, the long gray box was open and waiting.

My hands began to remember,
      the box was open and singing,
my hands,
      the box was open and humming one of them Indian songs,
my hands began,
      the box was open and whispering,
centuries began speaking to me.

Come closer, Grandson, we have been waiting for you,
he has been waiting for you,
Grandson, it is time to begin to finish.
It is time to break the circle, to make the circle new again.
It is time, Grandson, to rise up from the father highway,
to rise up and fly,
      for you are not he you are not he.
It is time to bury the man,
to find the father,
even if a father he could never be.
It is time to make it so,
to set yourself free,
      for you are not he you are not he.

The box was open and waiting.
I saw you.
It was election day
and my hands began to remember.

47

HANDS

Old man,
I stood over you in your box,
and when I reached to touch your gray folded hands,
I remembered, suddenly, a fair summer day beside big water,
when you laughed and lifted me
higher than the trees,

and I felt like a big boy,
I felt like a big boy,
in your hands I felt like a good boy,
and you said,
> *hey Chee-pwa,*
> *do you see any angels up there, do you see any angels?*

Old man,
I leaned over you in your box,
touched my hands into your thin gray wave of hair
and I whispered,
> *may the Grandfathers give you feathers, all is forgiven down here. . . .*

III

EXPLODING
CHIPPEWAS

We burn to a flash.

NO PIE

And I remember my mother's pearl-white hands
twisting the lid from her secret Mason jar. Her
pearl-white fingers pulling the silvery coins from
her secret Mason jar. A chilly day. We were going
off the rez, all the way to Bottineau, just to have
a piece of pie.

And I remember my mother's pearl-white fingers
tapping on the counter at the diner as we waited
to be waited on. Below the tall stool I knocked
together the dangling toes of my tattered sneakers.
The waitress ignored us until my mother said,
as sweetly as she could, *we'd like a piece of apple and
a piece of pumpkin, please.* The woman glared at us
from beneath the pile of her tilted hairdo, filterless
Pall Mall hanging from her cherried lips. *We are all
out of pie today,* she coughed. I glanced over at the
pie case, the fat pies lined up neatly behind the glass.
The woman hacked again, *we don't sell those pies by
the piece. Do you want to buy a whole pie?* My eye
twitched as my mother's pearl-white hand dipped
deep into the pocket of her coat, counting the
silvery coins.

And I remember my mother's pearl-white knuckles
trembling on the steering wheel as we crossed back
over the border. I knocked together the dangling
toes of my sneakers, staring at my small brown fists.
Her gaze was fixed hard on the road, while I turned
to watch the world speed by, both of our mouths
filled with tears.

MEANWHILE IN AMERICA

Big Tooth, the bottle prophet, once said to me,
very seriously, *you are lucky to be both Indian and white.*
That is, if it don't make you crazy.

And it is said that Grandma, scared of dying maybe,
rosary wrapped on her knuckles, once said, *I'm no dirty*
Indian, I tell you, I'm Italian. Jesus told me so.

Meanwhile, I'm eleven years old, fistfighting
my way back and forth to school each day. The
freckle-faced kids holler, *hey Chinese hey Chinese boy.*

Mother says it takes a bigger man to walk away.
I think about this as I erase where someone
has scribbled TONTO on my desk at school.

In the mirror my Indian hair sticks straight up.
The kids with cheeks the color of tomato
soup holler, *hey porky-pine hey porky-pine boy.*

I sleep each night with a tight cap made from my mother's
panty hose. Brylcreem in the mornings.

Alone in the white world, I sit and poke at the dirt
with a stick.

My friend Willie is the only one allowed to call me Chief.
I am the only one allowed to call him Cocoa. He says
to me, *at least you don't have to be black.*

I think about this as I erase where someone
has scribbled NIGGER LOVER on my desk at school.

My teacher speaks of history, so I ask, *why did the*
Europeans take away the Indians' land, anyway?
She pats me on my head, says, *well they didn't know*
how to take care of it, now did they?

Later, I was taught that we did not know how to take care
of our tongues, our minds, our ghosts, our children, anything
that we loved.

That summer back on the rez my cousins ask what happened
to my hair, and they say they're joking when they call me
white boy white boy.

Alone in the Indian world, I sit and poke at the dirt
with a stick.

WOMAN CALLS WATER

for S. K. Power

I

In a dream of mixed
blood memory I fall
toward the tear
that rests upon the cheek
of my Dakota grandmother.

I fall toward the tear that holds
the reflection
of my face,
where I see, past
my ear, over my shoulder,
a landscape that unfurls before
the rolling winds.

Freight trains burrow slowly
along the distant rails,
seeming to heatwave, melt
into the sky.

The great grasses ripple amber
to gold, dissolve into the curve
of earth, forever turning,
        forever scarred, healing
wound upon wound.

2

There were no ruts
before they brought the wheel, she says.
Only the cut of a hoof, the scratch
of the point of a stick
drawing circles within human circles,
hoops spinning, untangling to the sun.
There were no ruts
before they brought the wheel, she says.
The riverbank and shoulder
were strong before they brought
the wagons, before
the teams of oxen carried away
the humming, hissing skins
of all our brother buffalo.

3

I dive toward the tear
that falls along the cheek
of my Dakota grandmother.

I dive deep into the tear
that holds the river
of her remembering,
the river of our rage,
where a highway receding has cut
the heart, the circles of the land,
into maps and lines of longitude.

I swim within the tear
that crashes to the dust, followed
by another and another,

swelling to flood the plain,
to wipe away the dirt, then
bury all of our bones again.

4

The wheel is my enemy, she says.
The train is my enemy, the wagon, and the highway.
The map is my enemy, she says.
The wheel.

NOW WE SLEEP

INCA MAIDEN DEBUTS
—headline, *USA Today*, 22 May 1996

Now that you have found
our little southern sister
    (she was not lost),
at twenty thousand feet
upon a steep Peruvian slope,
frozen and crouching
to her knees, now
we sleep.

Now that you have told us
how she was sacrificed
    (she was given),
how wrapped and gently drugged
within her ceremonial dress,
primitive hands crashed
her skull against her brain, now
we sleep.

Now that you have counted
all of her beautiful teeth
    (you did not hear her whisper),
caressed her slender fingers,
measured the nails,
carved samples of tissue
from skin, bone, and breast, now
we sleep.

Now that you call her Juanita,
Inca maiden pure
        (we must name her La Molestada),
as you seal her inside your glass
refrigerated case, to place
her forever on display
to presidents and kings, now
we sleep.

Now we curl up, so civilized,
to join her
in the terrible dream
she has been given by you.

MABEL NEVER TELLS WHITE MEN SHE LOVES THE MOON

Imagine Mabel stands bent beneath the stars, her strong heart
echoing up the hills, her twisted cane
making circles in the air
to bless the moon.

Imagine all the fences, the highways, the bridges spanning
the empty Sea of Tranquility.

Imagine the mountains carved with the faces of our enemies.

Imagine Jane Fonda doing the tomahawk-chop from behind
her shades beneath a bubble
over a vast diamond of green.

Imagine the bulldozers smoking, digging up all those bones,
disturbing all those dreams.

Imagine the neon, the Golden Arches, the families four-wheeling
to Wal-Mart in their weightless Jeep Grand Cherokees.

Imagine the Man in the Moon marching down a new Trail of Broken Treaties.

Imagine Mabel stumbles on the path to the outhouse, under a moon
cluttered and dim, her twisted cane
tapping stones, earth,
roots of trees.

EDGAR TWO DOGS AND THE SINGING OF RAZOR BLADES

Each morning, as the god-damned
chirping of birds again drags
Edgar Two Dogs out of something that smells
remotely like sleep, he clamps closed
his eyes and reaches down to untangle
his testicles from sweaty sheets.
He pinches the wrinkled sack between
stained and jagged fingernails then curses
Gitche Manitou for failing to answer
his prayer to be crushed in the long night.

Edgar lifts himself to sit and sway
on the edge of the mattress, screws
off the cap of a half-empty bottle of Mad
Dog and serves himself the day's
first glorious gulp. He hopes that the holy
firewater will kill the worm curled
up in the rotten cavern of his top-left
molar, only to feel it jolt awake,
bite at the back of his tongue as it
refuses to ignite or even drown.

Edgar listens to the noisy worm gnaw
through the bone of his cheek
up into his skull to jitterbug in the soft
meat of his brain. The worm, mocking,
dangles its tail from his ear. The worm
slithers down the dried-out tunnels

of his veins, snickering in his heart.
The worm screeches and hollers,
shimmy-shimmy-shakes, twists
beneath the damp skin of his wrist.

Edgar rises to his purple, corn-pocked
feet, teeters, cracks and creaks, slowly
staggers to the bathroom, plops his ferocious
belly against the ice-cold sink. He heaves
forward to growl and spit at the blurry
potato of his reflection in the mirror.
He waggles out his tongue to charm or calm
the raucous worm, but he knows the only
way to set it free is to sing the old
rattle song of weeping, bleeding light.

Edgar listens to his fingers fumbling
through the medicine chest, the hollow
Q-tips box and the rusty toothbrush
tumbling to the greasy floor. The worm
quiets to feeding, a hungry hiss and hum.
Then Edgar hears the music of steel, sharply
sweet from beyond the torn curtain and,
with breath like moldy bread, he curses
Gitche Manitou for building the Tipi Bar
two blocks closer than the razor-blade store.

MY BLOOD IS BETTER THAN YOUR BLOOD

One says,
you are not Indian unless you grew up on a reservation, can speak your language, know the Traditional Ceremonies.

Two says,
you are not Indian if you have never hungered and happily eaten Government cheese, driven a one-eyed, rust-bucket car, been so drunk that you heard Geronimo singing on the radio.

Three says,
always remember that my bones are better than your bones.

Four says,
you are not Indian unless you grew up on a reservation before 1970, can name your clan, recite the Old Stories.

Five says,
you are not Indian if you have never thirsted and happily drank Government powdered-milk, had at least two hundred white people tell you about their Cherokee grandmother, been offered sex because you might be Indian.

Six says,
always remember that my skin is better than your skin.

Seven says,
you are not Indian unless you grew up on a reservation before 1940, you are a full-blood, your hair is jet black, thick, and straight.

Eight says,
you are not Indian if you have never wished that you weren't, been asked if you could make it rain, held your tongue when you wanted to explode.

Nine says,
always remember that my blood is better than your blood.

Ten says,
you are not Indian unless you grew up before reservations, you dreamed with Sitting Bull at Greasy Grass, you fell to your knees on the Trail of Tears.

Eleven says,
you are not Indian if you have never had your Indianness questioned by another Indian, been told to deny your white mother's blood, been lost and found and lost again.

Twelve says,
always remember that you will never be as Indian as me.

IN THE DREAM-ALL-NIGHT LAUNDROMAT

The old man passed out snoring,
tilting in the hard yellow
plastic chair against the window
of the all-night laundromat,
is dreaming again that he is
the young Indian boy he once
saw in a movie, war-whooping
wild and free across
the endless northern plain,
moon cool on his grinning
face, his bronze knees like lightning
bolts gripping the shiny
sides of a mad horse
made of wind and coming rain,

is dreaming again that he
is the young Indian man he once
saw in a movie, sweaty and brooding,
seducing the rancher's daughter
into the barn, lifting her heavy
skirts with his dirty hands,
her porcelain knees like lightning
bolts gripping his sides as she
twists and heaves to his pushing
her hard against a fragrant bale of hay,

is dreaming again that he
is the Indian man he never once
saw in a movie, strong and

64

sane, striking a smirk
from the face of John Wayne,
standing over the cowboy
in the dust and dung,
his leathery knees like lightning
bolts gripping the Duke's sides,
wrenching and breaking his spine,

is dreaming his last dream as he
explodes, spatters with blood
and wine the clattering, screeching
washing machines.

A VERY DISTANT DRUMMING

We could see the smoke for miles and we feared that we were next. We could see the smoke drifting up over the hills and it seemed that we could feel the heat of flame upon our skins. Our faces flushed and tightened. In my own mind I could see the flames, the long tongues wrapping all around the crooked shacks. The tongues licking in through the windows, eating up the curtains and chewing down the walls across the floors devouring the sad chairs, the sad leaning tables. In my own mind I listened to the long tongues but there was no sound. Everything was raging and quiet.

Silence. And I remembered my father's breath like a veil in the chilly air. He was pointing to the deer, the small buck standing at the edge of the clearing, sniffing and pawing at a patch of moss. His breath was like a veil as he motioned for me to be still, to listen. He lifted the bow, sited, then closed his eyes. I closed my own eyes, listening. I heard it very faintly, a very distant drumming. I heard it grow in my ears, or maybe in my belly. I heard it grow. It was a drum, so distinct that I could see the skin vibrating. I heard it grow, drum as distinct as a heartbeat, as true as a heartbeat. It was a drum so true that I could hear the blood push through. I could smell the meat of it, taste the life of it, true as a drum. And I could see, in my mind, its breath like a veil in the air. And I could feel my father's fingers let go the string let go the string and the drum was a heartbeat was a heartbeat stopped suddenly and there was nothing left but breath like a veil in the air. Silence.

In my own mind the long tongues silent. Flickering yellow snakes moving up and under the blankets into the beds, the sagging beds. Flickering tongue snake yellow snake winding its way beneath the blankets to quietly devour the fingers there. The dead fingers of those who slumped and coughed and twisted in their beds not knowing they were wrapping themselves in the disease. Not knowing they were. Not knowing. They were wrapping themselves.

We could see the smoke for miles and we feared that we were next. Standing in the snow, wrapped in our blankets, we listened. In my own mind I could see that there is nothing so black as that which has been burned. We could see the smoke for miles and we feared that they were coming. We listened for the horses, the turn of the wagon wheels. Standing there, together, our breath like a veil in the air.

EXPLODING CHIPPEWAS

The dark muscle of my heart
opens and closes
against their calling,
    when,
without sleep or warning,
the mothers and fathers
of my mothers and fathers
come to hum,
    to hover
and remind me of my blood.

In my head they say, *speak of us child,*
    remember us.

In my bones some of them weep,
strapped with their own braids
to slowly swinging crosses,
their meatless faces tight
with skin,

while others stomp down
the grass in quiet circles,
gripping shards of starry cloth
between their teeth,
    dripping
blood, white, and blue.

They burn to a flash,
a boom,

that sends me spinning,
    above, beneath, within
a forest of stars,
sky of trees.

2

Boom.
I wake to find myself
lying on my back
in the middle of my mother's
living room floor.
My eyes blur. Zoom in
zoom out, dart
from corner to corner to corner.
There is nothing to see.
There is only a buzzing,
the burning wick of a candle,
maybe the hiss of a dwindling fuse.

The first ghost appears as vapor
spinning out of the ceiling fan,
swoops over me once and twice,
crashes down on the arm of a chair
nearly toppling over.

The first ghost takes the shape
of a squatting man, a man perched,
long toes painted like silver
claws digging into the padded
arm of the chair.

The first ghost squawks and glares.
The pins of his narrow eyes
stab through the air.

The pins of his narrow eyes
screw into my chest.

The first ghost trembles,
lolls his head from side
to side, unruffles long, gray
hair down across the floor.
The thick tendrils wrap
tight around my bare feet.

The first ghost vibrates.
The pins of his narrow eyes
pierce the flesh of my heart.
The pins of his narrow eyes
spread open the dark muscle.

The first ghost does not speak
but I know his voice.
It is the sound of sunlight
dissolving, wings
unfolding over and over again.

The first ghost shudders
as my throat gurgles, mouth
floods with my own juice.
It is bitter and hot,
thick and rusty as iron.

The first ghost does not speak
but I hear the rush rattle
of his tongue plunging
into the wound. I feel
his salty tongue sopping
up my blood, clearing my throat,
seeking light.

I do not speak
but I know my voice.
It is the sound of moonlight
unraveling, water
lapping over and over again.

I veil, I drift, I fade away.

    3

Boom.
The second ghost appears as steam,
finds me somewhere in America
hunched over a tiny desk in a shabby
motel room, scribbling away the murky
hours before dawn,
before the moment
when I will rise from the chair
to begin another long day
on the oil-exploration crew,
before the moment
when I will gather
again with the other men
at a tilting table in the breakfast
joint next door to cough and grumble,
gouging the night from our eyes
over cups of thin coffee.

The second ghost appears as steam,
finds me hunched over, takes the shape
of a woman stepping out of the shower
shaking a stiff, white towel through
her bright blond hair,
the shape of a woman
crossing the room to press her

71

naked scent against my ear,
whispering over and
over the names of her Chippewa
grandmothers, the shape of a woman
crouching to drape her weary
lips around my faint
erection, dreaming that the ancient
ceremony of her sucking will
fill her smoky mouth with owl
wings, turtle shells, will save us both
from the moment when she will
again be the waitress pouring
cups of thin coffee for the coughing,
grumbling men gathered at the tilting
table in the breakfast joint
next door, gouging the night
from their eyes.

    4

Boom.
The third ghost appears as heat,
takes the shape of two thousand
swirling West Texas nights,
finds me leaning on the sticky
bar of another honky-tonk falling
madly in lust with another long
cowgirl. We will never touch
each other, really, we will never
reach each other, really, we will
never know each other at all,
finds me bending candlelight over
pen and paper. I will never write
anything, really, I will never
say anything, really, I will

never speak at all,
finds me driving the hard
bottom of the prehistoric sea
searching for any sign of my
family. Footprints, feathers,
blood. I will always be
looking, really, I will always
be lost, really, I will never
be found at all.
The third ghost appears as heat,
takes the shape of the northern
horizon, waving me home.

        5

Boom.
The fourth ghost appears as mist,
takes the shape of a young
man in a street-stained coat
plopping down in the empty
seat beside me as we barrel
down the bloody
throat of Chicago on the elevated train.

The fourth ghost raises the ax
of the edge of his hand,
splits open the petals of my
skull as we hurtle
down the bloody
throat of Chicago on the elevated train.

The fourth ghost bares the rusty
blades of his teeth,
scrapes out the dead flower of my
brain as we scream

down the bloody
throat of Chicago on the elevated train.

The fourth ghost peels away the wilted leaves
of my skin,
the fourth ghost peels away the dried-up leaves
of my flesh as we crash
down the bloody
throat of Chicago on the elevated train.

The fourth ghost carves one hundred
whistles from my bones,
blows a dusty
song as we disappear
down the bloody
throat of Chicago on the elevated train.

6

Boom.
The fifth ghost appears as light
on the shoulder of the woman
standing beside me in the sheltering
northern forest, appears as light
through the hair of the woman
swaying beside me on the smooth
edge of a powwow circle, appears as light
on the face of the woman
swooning beside me in the sacred
wisp of pine and cedar, appears as light
in the mouth of the woman
singing beside me in the breath
of the name of our first son.

The fifth ghost appears as light,
takes the shape of our fingers
entwined, appears as light,
takes the shape of our bodies
unfolding, appears as light,
takes the shape of her swollen
belly, appears as light,
takes the shape of a little boy
who dreams he flies, appears as light,
takes the shape of a little boy
who will run like the wind.

　　　　7

Boom.
The sixth ghost appears as breath,
takes the shape of the
word that is trapped in my
shoulder blade, is swollen
with ancient, sour blood,
is shaped exactly like a fist slowly
closing around the frantic
sting of a bee. It has the voice
of wings buzzing, collapsing.
It speaks of

the word that is lodged in the muscle
of my neck, is swollen
with ancient, sour blood,
is shaped exactly like a fist slowly
closing around the heavy breath
of a flower. It has the voice
of petals moaning, crushing.
It speaks of

the word that is caught in my
hair, is swollen
with ancient, sour blood,
is shaped exactly like a fist slowly
closing around the sad shake
of an eye. It has the voice
of lashes flitting, breaking.
It speaks of

the word that is hidden beneath
my scalp, is swollen
with ancient, sour blood,
is shaped exactly like a fist slowly
closing around the steady throb
of a memory. It has the voice
of light speeding, bending.
It speaks of

space tearing between
my folded knuckles,
speaks of time ripped open
against the tips of my fingers,
speaks of the shredded night
when she wept and shivered
on the porch of our house, my wife
grieving the name of our second son,
the snowflakes blinking, my cruel
hands dropping the blanket
over her head to somehow
hide the terrible terrible
sadness. The sixth ghost
takes the shape of the word

shaped exactly like *sorry*.
I was afraid of your sorrow, sorry.

I was afraid of your vanishing, sorry.
I was afraid of my weakness, sorry.
I was afraid our night would never
end, would go on spinning, sorry.
I was afraid I would leave, sorry.
I was afraid I would not return, sorry.
I was afraid of my fist, sorry.
I was afraid I would explode, sorry.

8

Boom.
I wake to find myself
lying on my back
in the middle of our bed.
My wife sleeps tight beside me.
My eyes blur. Zoom in
zoom out. My eyes dart
from corner to corner to corner.
There is nothing to see.
There is only a buzzing.
The burning wick of a candle,
maybe the hiss of a dwindling fuse.

The seventh ghost appears as smoke,
takes the shape of a child
wearing the face of my dead son.
He drifts into my arms,
rests his ear to the thump in my chest.
He reaches to touch my hands,
leans to kiss and forgive my fingers.

The seventh ghost curls,
wisps through his mother's hair,

caresses her cheek with his tiny lips.
He cradles her chin in his hands,
brushes her eyes with his breath.

The seventh ghost rises in the room.
He does not speak
but I know his voice.
It is the sound of light
exploding, hearts
expanding over and over again.

We burn to a flash
that sends us spinning,
reminds us of our blood.

ACKNOWLEDGMENTS

THANK YOU TO THE EDITORS of the following journals, anthologies, and chapbooks where these poems first appeared:

Cream City Review: "Meanwhile in America"

Dark Night Field Notes: "Now We Sleep"

Free Verse: "Flood," "In the Dream-All-Night Laundromat," "No Pie," "Orbit"

Laurel Review: "Draw," "Near"

LUNA: "Gravity," "Visitation"

Missouri Review: "Away," "Burn," "Grow," "Motion," "Signal"

North Dakota Quarterly: "A Very Distant Drumming"

Ploughshares: "Boom," "Call," "Tell"

Poetry: "Battlefield," "Reflection"

Power Lines: A Decade of Poetry from Chicago's Guild Complex (Tia Chucha Press): "Twist"

Prairie Schooner: "Exploding Chippewas," part 1, "Harvest," "Woman Calls Water"

Rattle: "Mabel Never Tells White Men She Loves the Moon"

Road Noise: A Poem (Mesilla Press): "Road Noise"

Seattle Review: "Go"

TriQuarterly: "Road Noise"

ABOUT THE AUTHOR

MARK TURCOTTE IS THE AUTHOR OF *Songs of Our Ancestors* (Children's Press, 1995), *The Feathered Heart* (Michigan State University Press, revised 1998), *Road Noise: A Poem* (Mesilla Press, chapbook, 1998), and *Le chant de la route* (Editions la Vague verte, bilingual, 2001), each illustrated by his wife, artist Kathleen S. Presnell. In 1993 he was winner of the first Gwendolyn Brooks Open-Mic Award. He was awarded the 1997 Josephine Gates Kelly Memorial Fellowship from the Wordcraft Circle of Native Writers and Storytellers and selected as a 1999 Literary Fellow by the Wisconsin Arts Board. He received a 2001–02 Lannan Foundation Literary Completion Grant. A member of the Turtle Mountain Band of Chippewa Indians, Turcotte lives in Fish Creek, Wisconsin, with his wife and son.